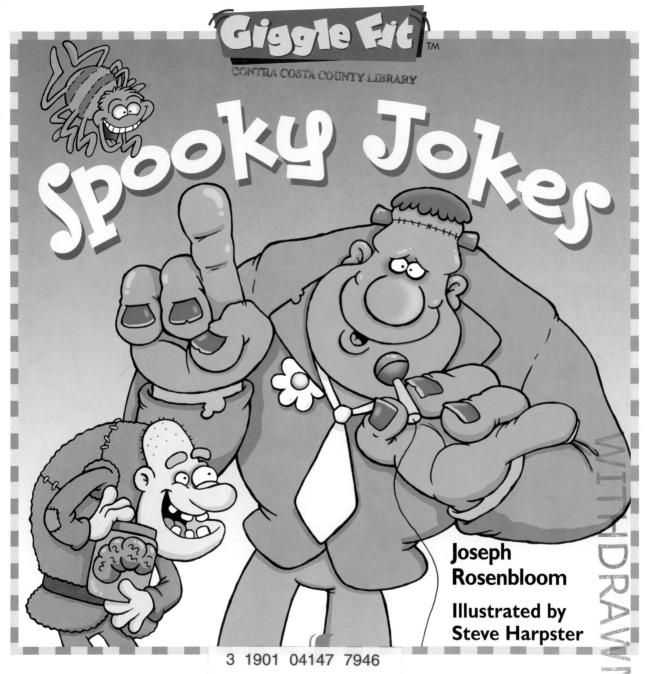

Giggle Fit™

Spooky Jokes

Joseph Rosenbloom

Illustrated by Steve Harpster

Sterling Publishing Co., Inc.
New York

Library of Congress Cataloging-in-Publication Data Available

10   9   8   7   6   5   4   3   2   1

Published in paperback 2004 by Sterling Publishing Co., Inc.
387 Park Avenue South, New York, N.Y. 10016
© 2003 by Sterling Publishing
Distributed in Canada by Sterling Publishing
^{c}/o Canadian Manda Group, One Atlantic Avenue, Suite 105
Toronto, Ontario, Canada M6K 3E7
Distributed in Great Britain by Chris Lloyd at Orca
Book Services, Stanley House, Fleets Lane, Poole BH15 3AJ, England
Distributed in Australia by Capricorn Link (Australia) Pty. Ltd.
P.O. Box 704, Windsor, NSW 2756 Australia
Printed in China

Sterling   ISBN 1-4027-0439-9   Hardcover
         ISBN 1-4027-1763-6   Paperback

What makes the letter G so scary?
It turns your host into a ghost.

What makes the letter W so surprising?
It turns your itch into a witch.

Why is the letter S so dangerous?
It turns lime into slime and makes cream scream!

Why do werewolves have fur coats?

Because they'd look silly in plastic ones.

How do you keep a werewolf from smelling?

Stuff up its nose.

What kind of fur do you get from a werewolf?

As fur as you can get.

How do you keep a werewolf from chewing up the back seat of a car?

Make it sit in front.

What does a werewolf do when traffic is snarled?

It snarls back.

How do you get fur from a werewolf?

By car, bus, train, or plane.

What goes "Ha-ha-ha—plop!"?
A monster laughing its head off.

What goes "Thud, thud, thud, squish"?
A monster with a wet sneaker.

What goes "Flap, flap, flap,
swoosh! Flap, flap, flap, swoosh!"?
**Count Dracula caught in a
revolving door.**

What is big, ugly, and goes
"Slam, slam, slam, slam"?
A four-door monster.

What happened to the woman who covered herself with vanishing cream?
Nobody knows.

What is more invisible than an Invisible Man?
The shadow of an Invisible Man.

Why can't the Invisible Man fool you?
Because you can see right through him.

Why did the Invisible Man look in the mirror?
To see if he still wasn't there.

When do monster mothers receive gifts?
On Mummy's Day.

Why couldn't the mummy answer the telephone?
Because it was all tied up.

What do mummies talk about when they get together?
Old times.

What has bandages and flies?
A mummy covered with jelly.

Why do mummies tell no secrets?
Because they keep things under wraps.

How can you tell if a mummy has a cold?
He starts coffin.

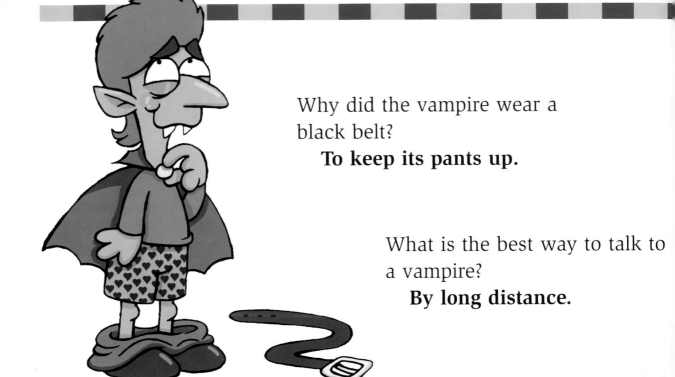

Why did the vampire wear a black belt?
To keep its pants up.

What is the best way to talk to a vampire?
By long distance.

What is the difference between a vampire with a sore tooth and a stormy day?
One roars with pain, the other pours with rain.

Where does a vampire keep its money?
In a blood bank.

How do you stop the pain of vampire bites?
Don't bite any.

Why should you avoid
vampires at dawn?
**Because they like a quick
bite before they go to bed.**

What would you get if you
crossed a vampire bat and a
magician?
A flying sorcerer.

What do you call a vampire that
faints at the sight of blood?
Unemployed.

What is gray, has big teeth, and prevents forest fires?
Smokey the Shark.

Why did the shark cross the ocean?
To get to the other tide.

Who lived in the ocean, had eight legs, and was a killer?
Billy the Squid.

How do sharks send messages through the ocean?
By Morse cod.

Why is a dragon big, green, and scaly?

If it were little, white, and smooth, it would be a Tic Tac.

How do you keep a dragon from going through the eye of a needle?

Tie a knot in its tail.

What has two blades and breathes fire?

A dragon on ice skates.

Which giant wore the biggest shoes?
The one with the biggest feet.

How do you get a giant
into a frying pan?
Use shortening.

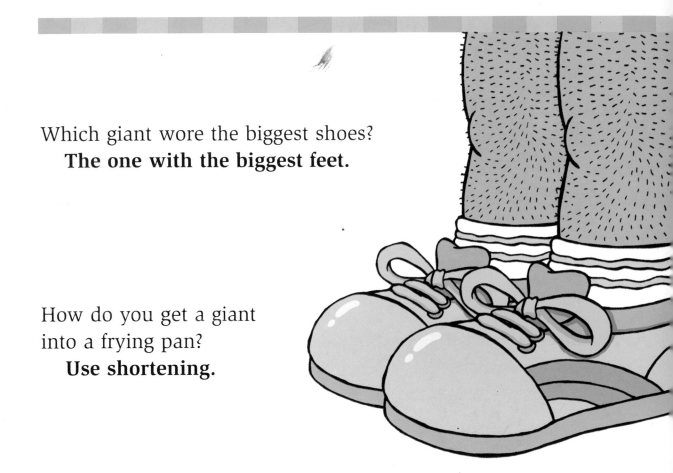

How do you get a giant into a pencil box?
Take the pencils out first.

How do six giants get out of a small car?
The same way they got in.

What would you get if you crossed a giant
and a computer?
A ten-ton laptop.

How do you get a giant out
of the cornflakes?
**Follow the instructions
on the box.**

What would you get if a rooster challenged King Kong?
Creamed chicken.

What's big and hairy and flies 1,200 miles per hour?
King Kongcorde.

What is King Kong's favorite flower?
Chimp-pansies.

How can you tell if King Kong has been in your refrigerator?

By the tracks in the butter.

Why did King Kong play with the flying saucer?

He thought it was a frisbee.

What time is it when King Kong knocks on your door?

Time to get a new door.

How long should a monster's legs be?

Long enough to reach the ground.

If three monsters are a crowd, what are four and five?

Nine.

What is a two-headed monster's favorite ball game?

A double-header.

What did the monster
eat after the dentist
pulled its tooth?
The dentist.

What monster comes
from New England?
A Vermont-ster.

What game do monster children play?
Hide-and-Shriek.

When do monsters remind you of creatures
from outer space?
When they're Martian along.

How does a witch tell time?
With a witch watch.

What is the first thing a witch rings for
in a hotel?
Broom service.

Why do witches fly brooms?
**Because vacuum cleaners
don't have long enough
cords.**

What is the most important
safety rule for witches?
Don't fly off the handle.

What does a witch say to
her broom at bedtime?
"Go to sweep!"

What do witches put on
their hair?
Scare-spray.

How does a witch travel when
she doesn't have a broom?
She witch-hikes.

Why is it hard to tell twin witches apart?
It's not easy to tell which witch is which.

How did the skeleton call home?
On the telebone.

What musical instrument does a skeleton play?
The trombone.

Why didn't the skeleton play church music?
Because he had no organs.

Why didn't the skeleton cross the road?
Because he had no guts.

How did the skeleton know it was raining?
He could feel it in his bones.

Why don't the police ever arrest skeletons?
Because it's hard to pin anything on them.

What branch of the service did the little phantom want to join when it grew up?
The ghost guard.

What's a ghost's favorite rock?
Tombstone.

On what day do ghosts make the most noise?
Moan-day.

What is the first thing that little ghosts learn in school?
Not to spook until they're spooken to.

What is a little ghost's favorite game?
Peek-a-BOO!

What is a little ghost's favorite
amusement park ride?
The roller ghoster.

What is a ghost's favorite
summer drink?
Ice ghoul lemonade.

What do you do when Godzilla sneezes?
Get out of the way.

What would you get if Godzilla stepped on Batman and Robin?
Flatman and Ribbon.

What would you get if you crossed Godzilla and a chicken?
The biggest cluck you ever saw.

What two things can't Godzilla have for breakfast?
Lunch and dinner.

How can you tell if Godzilla is in your lunch box?
The lid won't close.

What happened when Godzilla swallowed the chicken farm?
He was in a fowl mood all day.

Why does Godzilla eat raw meat?
He doesn't know how to cook.

What is Count Dracula's favorite sport?
Batminton.

Why did Count Dracula brush his teeth after every meal?
To avoid bat-breath.

Why is the Dracula family so close?
Because blood is thicker than water.

What would you get if you crossed a dog and Count Dracula?

I don't know, but its bite would be worse than its bark.

How can you tell if Count Dracula has been in your tomato juice?

By the two tiny tooth marks on the can.

Why did Count Dracula sleepwalk in his underwear?

He didn't have a batrobe.

When do zombies laugh?
When they make ghouls of themselves.

When do skeletons laugh?
When you tickle their funny bone.

Did Dr. Frankenstein make his monster laugh?
Yes, he kept him in stitches.

What would you get if you crossed a hyena and Count Dracula?
Someone who laughs at the sight of blood.

When is a vampire not a vampire?
When it turns into a haunted house.

How do you open a haunted
house?
With a skeleton key.

What is spookier than
the outside of a
haunted house?
The inside.

How can you tell if a monster is in bed with you?

There is an M on his pajamas.

Where do sea monsters sleep?

In water beds.

How can vampires go days without sleep and not feel tired?

Because they sleep nights.

What do you call a skeleton that sleeps all day?

Lazybones.

What's the best way to get rid of monsters in your dreams?
Wake up.

What can't you give a headless horseman?
A headache.

What did the Martian say to the gas pump?
"Take your finger out of your ear and listen to me!"

What does a zombie eat for breakfast?
Scream of Wheat.

What do ghosts eat
for breakfast?
Ghost Toasties.

When do ghosts eat
breakfast?
In the moaning.

What is green and
comes out at night?
Vampickle.

What would you call a
jittery sorceress?
A twitch.

What looks like a pickle, has a lot of teeth, and
lives in a swamp?
A crocodill.

What do ghouls eat in Chinese restaurants?
Misfortune cookies.

What happens when a banana sees a ghoul?
The banana splits.

Why did the giant eat two ducks and a cow?
He wanted quackers and milk.

What is yellow, smooth, and very dangerous?
Shark-infested mustard.

How do you make a strawberry shake?
Take it to a horror movie.

What does the Abominable Snowman eat for lunch?
Cold cuts.

What is worse than a vampire with a toothache?
An elephant with the sniffles.

What is worse than shaking hands with Count Dracula?
Shaking hands with Captain Hook.

What is worse than brushing a shark's teeth?
Removing its tonsils.

What is worse than a werewolf who needs rabies shots?
A vampire who needs braces.

What mummies live at the
North Pole?
Cold ones.

Where do mummies
swim?
In the Dead Sea.

What happens when mummies swim in the
Dead Sea?
They get wet.

What do mummies do on weekends?
They unwind.

What brings monsters' babies?
Frankenstork.

What is a monster's favorite holiday?
April Ghouls' Day.

How do you treat a scary monster?
With respect.

What do you call a witch doctor's mistake?
A voodoo boo-boo.

Where does a monster keep its hands?
In a handbag.

What do you do with a green monster?
Wait till it ripens.

What should you say to a
monster with no ears?
**Anything you want —
he can't hear you.**

Why doesn't it pay to talk to a
monster with four lips?
All you get is double talk.

How do you tell an elephant from a skeleton?
Wait for the wind to blow. The one with the flapping ears is the elephant.

How do you tell a zombie from peanut butter?
The zombie doesn't stick to the roof of your mouth.

How do you tell Count Dracula from a grape?
The grape is purple.

Why did Dr. Jekyll go to the beach?
To tan his Hyde.

Where does Dr. Jekyll
go to relax?
   To his Hyde-away.

Did you hear about the latest Dr. Jekyll and Mr. Hyde
miracle medicine?
   One drop and you're a new man.

When did Dr. Frankenstein stop being lonely?
When he learned how to make new friends.

What would you call a
monster's sweetheart?
His ghoulfriend.

Why did the Frankenstein
monster go out with a prune?
**Because he couldn't get
a date.**

How do you get in touch with
the Loch Ness monster?
Drop him a line.

Who do sea serpents date?
They go out with the tide.

What did the boy rattlesnake say to
the girl rattlesnake?
"Give me a little hiss."

Why do black widow spiders spin webs?
Because they don't know how to knit.

What is yellow, shoots webs, and jumps from building to building?
Spider-Banana.

What wears a black cape, flies through the air, and bites people?
A mosquito in a black cape.

What is green and wrinkled and goes through walls?
Casper, the Friendly Pickle.

How do you say goodbye to
Count Dracula?
"So long, sucker!"

How do you say goodbye to
a crocodile?
"See you later, alligator!"

How do you say goodbye to the
Abominable Snowman?
"Have an ice day!"

How do you say goodbye
to a two-headed monster?
"Bye-bye!"

INDEX